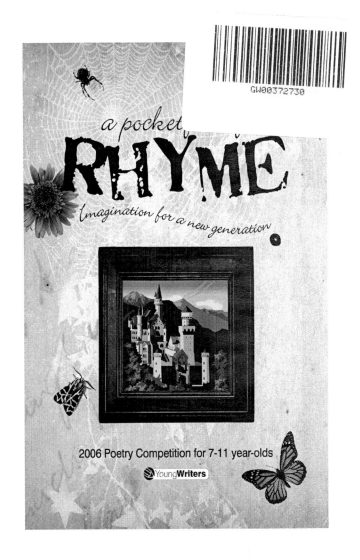

a pocketful
RHYME
Imagination for a new generation

2006 Poetry Competition for 7-11 year-olds

YoungWriters

Verses From Surrey
Edited by Mark Richardson

 Young**Writers**

First published in Great Britain in 2007 by:
Young Writers
Remus House
Coltsfoot Drive
Peterborough
PE2 9JX
Telephone: 01733 890066
Website: www.youngwriters.co.uk

SB ISBN 1 84602 742 X

Foreword

Young Writers was established in 1991 and has been passionately devoted to the promotion of reading and writing in children and young adults ever since. The quest continues today. Young Writers remains as committed to the nurturing of poetic and literary talent as ever.

This year's Young Writers competition has proven as vibrant and dynamic as ever and we are delighted to present a showcase of the best poetry from across the UK and in some cases overseas. Each poem has been selected from a wealth of *A Pocketful Of Rhyme* entries before ultimately being published in this, our fourteenth primary school poetry series.

Once again, we have been supremely impressed by the overall quality of the entries we have received. The imagination, energy and creativity which has gone into each young writer's entry made choosing the poems a challenging and often difficult but ultimately hugely rewarding task - the general high standard of the work submitted ensured this opportunity to bring their poetry to a larger appreciative audience.

We sincerely hope you are pleased with this final collection and that you will enjoy *A Pocketful Of Rhyme Verses From Surrey* for many years to come.

Contents

Asuka Hayashi (11)	21
Holly Stockham (7)	21
Greer Atkinson (9)	22
Stefano Carraro (7)	22
Hannah Gamber (8)	23
Joe Greenleaf (8)	24
Olivia Pipe (9)	24
Christian Milotte (8)	25
Kimberley Abbott (9)	25
James Chambers (8)	26
Amber Braysher (8)	26
Suavi Huseyin (8)	27
Luca Carraro (10)	27
Ben Smith (8)	28
Nabi Menai (11)	29
Ko Okuno (11)	30

Atwood Primary School

James Bell (8)	30
Liam Vickery (8)	31
Harrison Weaver (8)	31
Jessica Callaghan (8)	31
Geoffrey Niu (9)	32
Bekah King (8)	32
Rachel Douglas (9)	32
Gabriela Sachs (8)	33
Rosie Palmer (8)	33
Alexandria Bartolo (8)	33
Thomas Sutehall (9)	34
Mary Kelada (9)	34
Tom Combeer (8)	34
Kerry Allen (8)	35
Jacob Rolfe (9)	35
Venous Kanuga (8)	35
Madelene Cowley (8)	36
Stephanie Soosaipillai (8)	36
John-Paul Black (8)	36
Lauren Noone (9)	37
Bethany Reeve (8)	37

Bushy Hill Junior School

Tom Broomfield (9)	37
Bradley Welch (8)	38
Onika Khatun (10)	39
Thomas Bailey (10)	40
Charlotte Gallacher (11)	40
Christopher Murray (7)	41
Rosie Sandison (7)	41
Annie Sage (10)	42
George Cairns (10)	42
Angus Dunnett (10)	43
Robyn Jankowski (10)	43
Anya Murdoch (7)	44
Maduri Satkunabalan (10)	45
Chanice Raynbird (9)	45
Lucy Wolstencroft (8)	46
Rebecca McBean (10)	47
Georgia Bentham (8)	48
Sam Dean (8)	48

Greenvale Primary School

Daniel Cogswell (9)	49
Louis Hayes (9)	49
Jessica Newcombe (8)	49
Sophia Hinkley (9)	50
Caroline Francis (9)	50
Rebecca Thompson (9)	50
Nikhita Sharma (9)	51
Bethany Mills (9)	51
Max Smith (9)	51
Emily Tann (9)	52
Akash Harnal (9)	52
Sophie Langworthy (9)	52
Emily Lloyd (9)	53
Katie Standen (9)	53
Stefan Amokwandoh (10)	53
Katja Morris (9)	54
Victoria Brennan (9)	54
Lauren El-Bishlawi & Elle Westcott (8)	54
Mitchell Farrington (9)	55
Liam Jones (10)	55

St Catherine's Preparatory School, Guildford

Helena Dawes (9)	55
Megan Flint (9)	56
Georgia Leverett (10)	56
Ellie Backhouse (9)	57
Faith Browning (9)	57
Ellen Dixon (9)	58
Charlotte Owens (10)	59
Megan Lucas (9)	59
Arabella Pearson (9)	60
Christy Palmer (10)	60
Chloe Carruthers (10)	61
Ciara Milligan (10)	61
Freya MacAngus (10)	62
Annabelle Body (9)	62
Catriona May (10)	63
Natasha Allan (10)	63
Danielle Smith-Suarez (10)	64
Ellie Pilkington (10)	64
Abigail Ashby (11)	65
Maisie La Costa (10)	65
Georgina Steele (10)	66
Grace Richardson (11)	66
Megan Cowx (11)	67
Anna Lucas-Clements (10)	67
Ellen Bryden (10)	68
Lucy Barker-Hahlo (10)	69
Emily Fairweather (10)	70
Megan von Spreckelsen (10)	71
Libby Jeffery (10)	72
Helen Goldsbrough (10)	72
Victoria Schenk (10)	73
Milly Smith (10)	73
Lottie Palmer (10)	74
Lucy Courage (10)	75
Roseanna Windsor-Lewis (10)	76
Madelaine Salvage (10)	77
Katie Hillan (11)	78

St Peter's Primary School, South Croydon

Jordan Glass (10)	78

Maryam Haque (10)	79
Arrun Hawkins (10)	79
Amber Smith (10)	80
Ceilidh Harris (10)	80
Fenella Matlock (11)	81
Bethany Baden (10)	81
Grace Audus (7)	82
Ryan Sibbald (10)	82
Hope Bryan (7)	83
Zubair Amin (11)	83
Madeleine Wilson (10)	84
Lydia Hunter (9)	84
Reece Bage (9)	85
Joshua Mullins (9)	85
Joshua Anderson (7)	86
Anna Maria Loizou (10)	86
Charley Turner (9)	87
Leah Clifton-Dey (10)	87
Maggie May (9)	87
Kade Stroude (9)	88
Dean Chalk (9)	88
Amy Jones (9)	88
Thomas Thorne (9)	89
Amy-Jane Macartney (9)	89
Giorgia Fennell	89
Nicholas Peckham (9)	90
Beth Audus (10)	90
Andre Kennedy-Rodney (9)	90
George Dixon (9)	91
Connie Grant (9)	91
Jack Knights (9)	91
Thomas Sandle (9)	92
Sasha Vorontsov (7)	92
Taylor Sidney (8)	92
Ashleigh Stevens (7)	93
Samuel Ave (8)	93
Sade Parker (9)	93
Cameron Warr (7)	94
Amira Zerrouki (9)	94
David Mincer (9)	94
Mya Douglas (7)	95
Georgia Clifton-Dey (8)	95

George Lawrence (7)	95
Rebecca Audus (7)	96
Daphiene Reid (8)	96
Kye Clarke (8)	97
Ellé Barker (8)	97
Kelem Tahir (8)	98
Jack Murray (8)	98
Maia Desaa (8)	99
Hannah Pettengale (8)	99
Chloe Lewis (8)	100
Hannah Darkes (9)	100
Max Nichols (7)	100
Elsa Hunter (7)	101
Thomas W F Dixon (7)	102
Sashawne Smith (7)	103
Anna Mapstone (7)	104
Hannah Penn (7)	105
Lucy Taylor (7)	106

The Poems

Summer

The colour has exploded,
Everywhere you can reach,
The sun is really shining,
The warmth touching your feet.

I really love the summer,
It really is a treat!
The flowers have just risen,
They all smell very sweet!

The birds are singing happily,
Up in the old oak tree,
The grass as soft as ever,
As green as it could be.

The sun has just started setting,
It's time for me to sleep,
'Goodnight, sweet dreams,' I say,
As I fall asleep!

Surina Mawkin (10)
Aberdour School

Hollie And Molly

There was a young girl called Hollie
Who thought herself very jolly
She fell out of bed
And bumped her head
And forgot her best friend was Molly
Molly got sad
And Hollie was glad
Until she realised she had no friends
The egg on her head
Had made her different she said
And became Molly's best friend again.

Hollie Braysher (8)
Aberdour School

Candyfloss Dreams

I get home from school
And lie on my bed,
I try to rest my sleepy head.
I lie there just thinking,
Thinking of things,
Thinking of my favourite thing.

Candyfloss that would be . . .
So soft and fluffy, as sweet as can be.
I put out my arms and reach for the clouds,
I'm in a deep sleep with candyfloss now.

I go to feel it in my dream,
It's so soft and sticky, squidgy it seems.
I go to smell it, it smells so sweet,
The smell has knocked me off my feet.
I go to taste it, it just melts in my mouth,
It's so delicious,
But it looks just like clouds.

Instead of white, there's pink, blue and green,
With that taste, that smell, that look so clean.
It's making me want to dream and dream,
But suddenly, I'm woken up,
My mum is calling me for my tea.
Please Mum! Candyfloss for me!

Lilli Crossley (9)
Aberdour School

Frosty

Frosty mornings, icy snow,
It's what I see from my window.
I dress up warm then give a shout,
To let Mum known I'm going out.
I want to be the first you know,
To put my footprints in the snow.

Raymond Higgins (7)
Aberdour School

Wrestling Poem

I would like to be a Smackdown wrestler
But my mummy said *no way!*
I'm going to try and convince her
And this is what I've got to say!

Wrestling's not *that* violent, it's exciting and too much to call
If I were ever in the ring, I'd stand at 20 feet tall
To watch it though, you'll need Sky Sports Three
And you could watch the world champion that I will be.

People cheer and clap at every move I make
Especially when I jump and spin and the dodging that I take
No contender will ever match my awesome pace
The world champion belt will be hanging round my waist.

My favourite tag-team partner would be The Undertaker
It's best to be friends with him or he'll take me to my maker
I try and watch it every Friday night to try to get some tips
Unless my mummy hears me and then she'll do some flips.

I would like to be a Smackdown wrestler
But my mummy said *no way!*
Do you think I have convinced her?
I don't think so, what do you say?

William Sturdy (8)
Aberdour School

The Lucky Pup

There once was a pup that lived on the street,
He almost had no heartbeat.
Then came a boy without any sin,
Who picked him out of the trash bin.
He kept him as his pet and cleaned him up,
Now he lives the life of a normal pup.
Thanks to this boy, this pup didn't die,
But now he's eating apple pie.

Thomas Bradbury (10)
Aberdour School

My Favourite Ponies

I like to ride on Pepper,
He's really, really fast,
I like riding around the riding school
And also on the grass.

There is another horse called Scout,
He is sometimes very slow,
But if I hit him with my crop,
He can really, really go.

Poppet is a sweetie,
But very, very small,
But even is she canters off,
I will never ever fall.

Matilda is my favourite pony,
She is bigger than the rest,
She trots very well,
That's why she is the best.

Connie Godden (7)
Aberdour School

Chardonnay

I have a little chicken
Her name is Chardonnay
She lives with my auntie
A long way away
Her feathers are brown
And her head is black
Freshly picked broccoli
Is her favourite snack
She pecks around the garden on her skinny little legs
We hope that sometime soon she will start to lay some eggs
I love my little chicken
Whose name is Chardonnay
How I wish that she didn't
Live quite so far away.

Eleanor Musgrove (9)
Aberdour School

My Two Cats

My pet Mischief
I'm sorry to say he's a bit of a thief.
Whenever we leave food on the table,
He jumps up and eats what he's able.
He's black and white,
He's quite a sight.
He's rather fat,
He loves his mat.
He has a sister, Charlie,
Who's sometimes rather snarly.
She's Mischief's twin,
She's really thin.
She's as quick as a fly,
She's rather shy.
She's quite a cat!
And I love her
And Mischief.

Fraser Watt (9)
Aberdour School

My Holiday

Finally, we were on the plane,
I had time to memorise its name,
Ten delays all one hour each,
But all worth it when on the beach.
Sailing, swimming, volleyball too,
To name just a few,
Eight weeks all flew by,
I really must ask why.
Why time flies when you're having fun,
But slows when you're having none?
Now I'm back
And all seems black.

Christopher Huber (11)
Aberdour School

My Baby Sister

My baby sister is as cute as can be
At 5 weeks, all she could do was smile at me

Time flies and she has grown so fast
Soon she will be reaching up to my knees

At 15 weeks she laughs and sings
When I'm away at school I miss her grin

At 25 weeks she sits with me
Grabs my toys and plays with me

I love my baby sister
Her tiny toes and chubby cheeks

She will always be my favourite
No matter how old or naughty she might be.

Ameer Menai (8)
Aberdour School

The Solution To Pollution

Pollution! Pollution!
Here is the solution.

Litter! Litter!
It makes me so bitter.
Don't be such a grump,
Throw it in the dump.

Smoke! Smoke!
It makes me choke.
Gas and oil smell,
Use wind and water as well.

Lazy! Lazy!
Everyone's crazy.
Lend a hand
And you'll save our land.

Ben Hibbitt (9)
Aberdour School

Seasons

Summer is when the sun shines and makes you very hot,
With deckchairs out and suncream on, I like it such a lot.
When it's such a sunny day and all you want to do is play,
You go out for a picnic on a Saturday.

Autumn is when the country is covered with red, yellow and gold,
Leaves are fluttering in the wind and are falling bright and bold.
The days are getting shorter and the nights are getting dark,
Soon it will be time to wrap up warm for that bike ride in the park.

Winter is when the snow starts falling,
Getting colder and colder every morning.
Children build snowmen with funny faces
And then have exciting downhill races.

Spring is when the flowers start growing,
Crocuses, daffodils and tulips start showing.
Cute little lambs are being born,
Another year is about to dawn.

Holly Sharman (9)
Aberdour School

Holiday In The Maldives

A deserted island in the clear blue sea,
I'm snorkelling swiftly through the coral, feeling free,
Multicoloured fish, yellow, blue and stripy zebras, all following me.

There ahead, like a colossal red whale,
A sunken wreck sleeping in peace, where its captain had failed,
Black holes show me where the rocks have impaled.

Back in the speedboat, racing along,
Searching for dolphins and listening for their song,
There! There they are! No, now they've gone!

Tired now, lying in my hammock under a palm,
Waves surge and hiss, making me calm,
Let me stay here forever, safe in nature's arms.

Nicholas Taffinder (9)
Aberdour School

My Little Sister Sarah

My little sister Sarah,
Is always messing around,
When she gets excited,
She jumps off the ground.
When she gets told off,
She has a little frown,
When I play with her,
She always bosses me around.
My little sister Sarah.

My little sister Sarah,
Can sometimes be a star,
She wakes me up in the morning with a hug
And crawls around like a bug.
When we go out to the park,
She wants to stay out till it's dark,
She waves goodbye to me at school
And welcomes me with treats in the afternoon.
My little sister Sarah,
I like her a lot,
When she breaks up my train tracks,
I go mad and wish she went in a magic pot.
My little sister Sarah.

Adam Shakir (6)
Aberdour School

My Idol

M y idol is the best, she always wears a vest
Y oung and good looking, hardly reads books

I f she was on stage, she would never make a rage
D isco parties all night - tries to grab a quick bite
O ff next morning, always yawning
L ondon is her funky town, always wears her lucky gown.

Pascale Mama (8)
Aberdour School

My Imaginary Brother Blue

My imaginary brother Blue
He's only twenty-two
He likes to collect sticks
And even bricks

He's even got a sailing crew
Which he drew
He's got a green pen
And he even drew a dog's den

He doesn't like cats
But he loves rats
He gets in a muddle
And once he jumped in a puddle
He's really dumb
But he's so much fun
He's very tall
And his favourite toy is a ball

He's a good plumber
And his car is a Hummer
He's a good drummer
And a good imaginary brother.

Sam McDonald (8)
Aberdour School

My Great Grandma, My Great Friend

My great grandma Maureen lived by the sea,
She always told me stories about my mum and Uncle Lee.
She always gave me a Ribena and a Milky Bar,
And we would go for a walk, even though she could not go far.
She liked to watch me throw stones in the sea,
By the look on her face, she was as happy as could be.
She like fried onions in her burger and chewing gum after her tea,
My great grandma Maureen who lived by the sea.

Kai Bowers (8)
Aberdour School

My Fish

I have two fish called Sun and Cloud,
They are very joyful and fun to have around.

Sun is bright and quite small,
Cloud is grey and not small at all.

Cloud is big with a patch on top,
Sun is gold and likes to eat a lot.

Those two play games around the clock,
Hide-and-seek in the plants and rock.

They wave their fins when they swim,
It's food time, so they come up to the brim.

They come up for their flakes of food,
It puts them in a very good mood.

During the day they swim very deep
And at night-time they fall asleep.

I love my fish, I tell them out loud,
I love my fish, Sun and Cloud.

Max Hawkins (7)
Aberdour School

Autumn

Wrap up warm,
Jumpers, coats and hats,
Hallowe'en is coming,
Pumpkins, masks and bats.

Raking up the leaves,
Conkers falling off the trees.
It's nippy and chilly,
Run about and be silly.

Colours of gold, yellow and red,
A big mug of hot chocolate,
And then off to bed!

Jack Beard (9)
Aberdour School

Seasons - My Favourite Things

Spring
Daffodils opening, baby lambs born
Bird eggs hatching, weather is warm
Spring showers make sure of blossom on trees
Mum, can I wear my Wellingtons, please?

Summer
Hot, lazy days when the sun is shining
Asleep on the deck, ice cream melting
Strawberry picking, yummy to eat
Bikini on body, flip-flops on feet.

Autumn
Morning mist, conkers, berries grow on trees
Walks in the forest, crackling, golden leaves
Bonfires burning, fireworks display
I wish I could go and play in the hay.

Winter
Scarves and mittens, hats and coats
Frost outside, sometimes even snow!
Toasted muffins and crumpets by the fire
Christmas presents to admire.

Charlotte Collins (8)
Aberdour School

The Tiger

A tiger is prowling through the jungle,
He doesn't know that a hunter sees him.
The hunter aims his gun to shoot,
But a lion cub sees the hunter's shoes.

The lion pulls the hunter's leg,
Making the hunter lose concentration.
The tiger growls and turns away,
Safe, well anyway, for today.

Hannah Brown (10)
Aberdour School

My Holiday

I went to my holiday house in Majorca for the whole of the summer.
It was a scorcher.
We swam in the clear blue sea, my mummy, daddy, brother and me.
We went on my daddy's boat, but certainly did not need a coat.
I got stung by a jellyfish, what a fright!
I swam back to the boat with all of my might.
We went to the water park with Jo and Sam and raced down the
slalom slides, one, two, three, go,
We went to Marineland to watch the dolphin show and saw the
sea lions dancing, we laughed, ho, ho, ho.
As the weeks rolled on and the sun still shone,
My friends Megan and Harrison came and we played on and on.
We went on the banana boat and surfed in the sea,
Played on the beach making sandcastles, before going home for tea.
It was such great fun to be so free,
Next year I am going to learn how to waterski.

Oliver Noble (8)
Aberdour School

My Friends

My friend Bethany is very smart
She knows her 12 times table off by heart.

My friend Rachel is sporty and fast
She's always running around and never comes last.

My friend Hannah plays the flute
It's a lovely sound and it makes her look cute.

My friend Lucy is on the school council
She likes it really, but prefers to play netball.

I have lots of friends at school, but by far
My best friend is my little sister Jessica!

Caitlin Penn (8)
Aberdour School

Me And My Cats

Monty is my grown-up kitten, he's round and very fluffy,
He is stripy, grey and white and sometimes can be scruffy.
He's often very cheeky and he climbs up people's legs,
When he's feeling hungry, he looks at his bowl and begs.
He runs across the garden, he chases after balls,
He's good at climbing fences, but he's not so keen on walls.

Millie is a silver tabby, she's small and very fat,
She has a very curly tail and never keeps it flat.
Sometimes she hunts for birds and mice, and spiders too are
                                              very nice,
But mostly Millie stays indoors, curled up and snoozing on her paws.
At night she chases after moths, leaping, twisting and turning,
By day she is a lazy thing, she even gets me yawning.

I love my cat called Monty, he's the perfect cat for me,
But with his sister Milly, we're a family of three.

Katie Grimstone (9)
Aberdour School

My Pet

My little bunny is so funny
Grazing on grass and moss,
She jumps about without a pout
Springing to and fro.

She likes to run in the hot, hot sun
Racing through the garden,
But in the night she sleeps so tight
Hiding in her hutch.

Her meals are very tasty
Chewing hay and corn,
Her favourite food is carrot
Eating snacks all day.

Patrick Huber (10)
Aberdour School

Golf Is The Game!

He prowls on the course ready for play,
He's praying he's going to win on this day.
For he is the Tiger, the best of them all,
He focuses hard as he strikes the ball.

Golf is the game
Where he found his fame,
Tiger Woods is his name,
There is no one the same!

As he approaches the tee, deep in thought,
Well aware there's a battle to be fought,
He looks at the pin in the distance far,
Hoping to score this hole below par.

Golf is the game
Where he found his fame,
Tiger Woods is his name,
There is no one the same!

Smack, with a strike the ball flies through the air,
It lands in a bunker - the Tiger glares.
With a neat little chip, the ball drops on the green,
A putt and the ball's holed for all to be seen.

Golf is the game
Where he found his fame,
Tiger Woods is his name,
There is no one the same!

Sebastien Carpenter (9)
Aberdour School

Holidays

Until I broke my leg,
My holiday was great!
I was in a lot of pain,
But I hung out with my mate.

I was boarding in the sea,
Having lots of fun.
I threw my board onto the wave
And landed on my thumb.

I hit the ground with a great big thump
And yelled out to my dad.
He looked and said, 'That looks broken!'
I was really, really sad.

I went to the clinic and saw a doc,
Who shook his head and said,
'Oh no dude, a broken leg!'
And made me stay in bed.

They put me in a bright green cast,
Which hurt from toe to thigh,
They gave me crutches and a wheelchair,
A happy boy? Not I!

For me, however, the best thing was,
Flying home in style!
They put me in a first class seat,
So I wouldn't block the aisle.

Matthew Godden (11)
Aberdour School

My Pony

My beautiful white pony is called Teddy
When I want to ride, he is always ready
We trot or canter and can jump poles together
He takes me safely, whatever the weather

His muzzle is soft as velvet
Like the blue cover on my helmet
We ride up the hills and love to roam
But when it's time, he takes me home

I took him to the beach for the holiday
He went in the sea and loves to play
We cantered on the sand and laughed all the way
Once we were home, he had a treat of hay

He loves to eat carrots and apples
When his whiskers touch my hand, it tickles
He always tries his best for me
That's why I love Teddy.

Abigail Tudor (9)
Aberdour School

My Hamster

My hamster is golden-brown, his paws are bright pink
And he follows me around.

He runs on his ball and scurries on his wheel
And sunflower seeds are his favourite meal.

He's cute and cuddly and I love him very much,
He's fun to play with and soft to touch.

I feed my hamster every day,
I give him food and water in his hay.

I clean out his cage once a week
And he sits there watching me with a bit of apple in his cheek.

At night-time when I go to sleep,
My dreams are full of his pitter-patter feet.

Lucy Upot (9)
Aberdour School

Sweet Sibling

What a marvellous surprise
When my lovely baby sister arrived!

When I saw her face
Delight danced in my eyes!

Her smile is so wide
She always gets on her brother's good side.

In the morning she comes bobbing into my room
Spreading cheer all round, ridding it of all gloom.

Time flies fast when I'm caught in her spell
Is that my enchantress and her baby powder I smell?

Soon it is dinner time, based strictly on milk
Bath time, pink PJs, all wrapped up in silk.

A quick kiss goodnight
A snuggle with Marcelle, the silk clown.

She's fast asleep now
Shush, not a sound!

Vali Menai (9)
Aberdour School

My Special Holidays

Summer in the Alps
We walked down the Alps
There were lots of butterflies
The grass was a carpet of green
It was the most beautiful place I had ever seen

Winter in the Alps
We skied down the mountain
I forgot to go into snow plough
I came really fast down the black
I got to the bottom and fell on my back!

Yasmin Davies-Nash (9)
Aberdour School

My Holiday

We pack our cases excitedly,
With T-shirts, shorts and hats.
We've got to make more room though,
To take our cricket bats.

The airport is really busy,
With bustle and noise.
We can take books to read,
But Mum says, 'No toys!'

It's a long way to go,
To the sea and the sand.
Up and up the plane goes,
Away from dry land.

Mickey Mouse is waiting for us
And dolphins in the sea.
The sun is shining brightly,
This is the life for me!

Tom Beard (9)
Aberdour School

The Countryside In Summer

Great green hills and
Big blue skies with
Fluffy white clouds that float quietly by.

Sunny woods and
Country roads,
Where we're going
No one knows.

Birds that tweet
In trees up high,
As they fly in the summer sky.

Just look at the beautiful countryside
With all its secrets
And places to hide.

Hannah Taylor (9)
Aberdour School

My Imaginary World

My imaginary world,
It's up in space,
It's better than winning any race.
It's in the fog,
Under a mossy, green log.
It's in Mars,
With lots of cars.
Far, far, far,
I saw a star,
From my imaginary world.
Quick! Someone's coming!
I'd better start running.
Who could be there?
Could it be a bear?
A dreadful hullabaloo,
It sounds like beep-boo.
It's just my alarm going *beep, beep,*
What a jolly good relief!

Lily Upot (8)
Aberdour School

Battle On The Beach

From the boat we saw some smoke.
Through the water we tried to reach the beach,
The soldiers were having trouble.

The German guns were shooting,
We hid behind a rock.
We breached them at the bunker
Because we had good shots.

Through the forest we did run,
We nearly lost our guns.
We threw grenades and they exploded,
Capturing the fort.

Markus Huber (7)
Aberdour School

A Day At The Zoo

Go to the zoo for a brilliant day,
Where you can watch the animals having a play.
The monkeys are here, the tigers are there,
All kinds of animals, common and rare.

Look at the elephants big and strong,
Playing in the mud and lying in the sun.
Being hosed down while waiting for lunch,
They are now hungry, *munch, munch, munch.*

It's feeding time in the reptile house,
The snakes are hungry, so watch out little mouse.
The frogs are croaking, swallowing lunch,
Look at them, a happy bunch.

At the end of the day it is time to go home,
The keepers are pleased, but young children moan.
Parents are tired - the animals too!
Preparing for tomorrow when the fun will continue.

Thomas Earl (9)
Aberdour School

Holidays

Holidays are great fun
Even if it's hot in the sun
I love to play in the sand
But I also like to play on land
The water is always so cool
And much better than being at school.

I always make new friends
But I hate it when it ends
I always go to bed late
When I'm with my new mate
Soon it's time to go back
And I'm packing up my sack.

But it was great fun on holiday!

Kirsty Hume (7)
Aberdour School

My Favourite Pet

My favourite pet
Dark brown, silly pet
He has two kinds of ball
He always kicks it and makes it roll
And bites and eats his wooden ball

When he feels slightly bad
Sitting on his straw bed
When he needs lots of food
He kicks the ball, bites his friend
Shows he needs lots of food

He moves his nose every time
Playing around every time
Sleeps at noon, wakes at night
My favourite pet
My dark brown bunny, silly pet.

Asuka Hayashi (11)
Aberdour School

My Pet Rules

My cat loves to play in every way,
When it's cloudy, he doesn't care,
But it might give him a *nightmare!*

But whatever the weather,
I do have to say,
He's always hungry,
So we have to buy his food every day.

But does he get full up?
I feel the answer is no,
Because my cat is always on the go.

My cat wears a hat and a tie,
He's always happy,
So he will never cry.

Holly Stockham (7)
Aberdour School

My Precious Pet

I have a dog called Fluffy
And she is a puppy,
She plays with her balls
And paddles in the pond,
Oh, what a laugh she is!

When I walk Fluffy to school,
We always go in the field,
She runs around like mad
And I run along with her.
Oh, what a laugh she is!

When I feed Fluffy,
I put treats in her bowl,
She's such a rascal,
She goes fishing for them all.
Oh, what a laugh she is!

When I put Fluffy to bed,
She's a struggle to get in,
But soon she dozes off,
Oh, I love her so much,
My precious pet,
Shhh!

Greer Atkinson (9)
Aberdour School

Stan

Stan the man
He is a Chelsea fan.

He sits in the stands
And shouts and waves his hands
And when John Terry scores
He roars and roars.

Stefano Carraro (7)
Aberdour School

My Cute Brother

My brother is very cute
But sometimes he is annoying

He is very playful
But not so careful

He pinches and scratches
And leaves sticky patches

In the evenings he definitely
Hates having his socks and shoes taken off

He has a real tantrum
Oh, yes he does

He loves eating, you should see how much
He tries to eat whatever he can touch

When you wrap presents up
He crinkles all the wrapping paper up

He's a right cheeky boy
He's a cheeky monkey too

He dances to my music
And looks quite funky

He does handstands and flips over
With my help, of course

I try and help him say words
But he can't say very many

I help him build towers with his blocks
But he knocks them down

I help him read
But he just points at the dog

I love my brother although
He does all these cheeky things.

Hannah Gamber (8)
Aberdour School

Happy Families

There are four of us in our family,
Mum, Dad, Lucy and me.
My sister is annoying,
But she says the same about me!

I've got lots of aunties and uncles,
But they live quite far away.
Some of them are in Ireland
And sometimes they come to stay.

I've only got one nana,
She's very kind and nice,
But I have an extra grandpa,
Because Nana got married twice!

We are a very happy family,
Most of the time,
Sometimes we get mad with each other,
But we usually get on fine.

Joe Greenleaf (8)
Aberdour School

My Favourite Pet

Slowly he peeps out of his shell,
Is that lettuce he can smell?
One leg first, then another,
His head stretches out a little further.
He has small black eyes and a little nose,
He burrows in the sand to have a doze.
His shell is round with a pattern on the top,
A bath full of water makes him stop.
He has a best friend called Daisy,
Who sometimes drives him crazy!
He's my pet tortoise called Tom.

Olivia Pipe (9)
Aberdour School

Make-Believe

When I was young
I had a dream
I went to a faraway place

When I was young
I had a friend
His name was Benoit

When I was young
We used to play fun games
We would build blocks as high as the sky

There was always someone to talk to
Always someone to fly planes with

I remember the friendship
And the fun times
When I grew up
I wished I could remember the young times.

Christian Milotte (8)
Aberdour School

My Precious Pets

My dogs are called Abby and Claire,
They love to munch on wood as much as they dare!
Abby and Claire are very naughty,
But always up and sporty!
They like me to throw sticks
And sometimes they find bricks!
They try to jump on the trampoline,
But fail sadly with a scream!
They look in the windows of the swimming pool
And then run around the garden like fools.
One morning out for a walk,
They looked at me as if they could talk.
But at the end of the day when they fall in a pile,
I know I go to bed with a smile.

Kimberley Abbott (9)
Aberdour School

Autumn Fears

Autumn is a scary season
Dark nights and trick or treating children
In the street shadows are moving everywhere
Strange noises outside my bedroom door

Downstairs there are pumpkins
Frightening faces and candlelight
Black cats, bats and spiders
Cobwebs dangling and screams of terror

Peeping from my hiding place
I can see skeletons dancing
Witches are trying to fly
Ghosts and monsters are freaking me out

Are these monsters from my imagination
Or my sister's Hallowe'en party friends?

James Chambers (8)
Aberdour School

Sleepy Dreams

When I go to sleep
I always dream
Of beautiful places
I have been to see
Of rivers and lakes
And places to skate
In a winter wonderland
Of catching leaves
When they fall from trees
And sailing my boat
Without getting soaked
I wake up so happy
After such a good dream
I can't wait to go to sleep again!

Amber Braysher (8)
Aberdour School

My Brother

You'd love to squeeze your teddy
You'd love to squeeze your mum
But the only thing you wouldn't want to squeeze
Is my little brother.

His bones protrude all over his body
Which does not make him so cuddly
And why is he like this, you'd say
Simply because he skimps his three meals a day

The cutest thing about him though is
His Bambi eyes so brown and wide
His eyelashes are like spider legs
Which always brings him great attention
Have I forgot to mention
That he is really very funny?

So, overall he's skinny and sweet
And you will instantly recognise him when you meet.

Suavi Huseyin (8)
Aberdour School

Otto

We have a cob horse called Otto
He goes to lots of shows
He wins lots of prizes
Because he goes and goes.

He is a strawberry roan
He likes to wander and roam
He eats lots of mints
And his favourite type are Smints.

He is really cute
But if you put a foot wrong
He'll tread on your boot
So look down below
And you won't get a bruised toe.

Luca Carraro (10)
Aberdour School

My Pet's Friends

My pet has friends
They don't use pens.
There's Potty Penguin and
Mad Mouse
Crazy Cat and
Groovy Goldfish
But their best friend
Is Daft Dog
He's a cool kid
Who is as mad as a lid.

Daft Dog
Has a log
Under the log
There is a hog
A bog
A bug
A mug
But nothing
Surprises doggy, doggy
Doggy Dude.

Potty Penguin likes
Clever Cat
Clever Cat likes
Groovy Goldfish
But their best friend
Is . . . *Daft Dog*
Mad Mouse doesn't like
Clever Cat because he
Goes . . .
Pounce.

Ben Smith (8)
Aberdour School

Happy Seasons

In autumn I play in the colourful leaves,
All the colours that come down from the trees

On a bright, sunny day in fall,
Outside I wander until it's cold and dark

In winter I play in the snow,
When the flowers don't grow

I am in a winter wonderland,
Making a snowman

The trees are no longer bare
New colours and hues have filled the air

I know spring is on its way,
I can hear the cardinals and the blue jay

On a hot summer's day,
All my brothers and I play

And when I want to be cool,
I go with Dad to the pool

Wow, I never knew,
Seasons were so great!

Nabi Menai (11)
Aberdour School

Vampires

Drip . . . blood . . .
Vampire sucking blood,
Drying out bodies,
Baring his fangs,
Waiting for your blood!

Having bats as their assistant,
Killing their breath,
In the darkness of the
Hidden habitat of
The hunters . . .

Living nightmare,
Vampire,
Vampaneze,
Vampirates,
How many are there?

Are you scared?
No?
OK, how about if I say,
'It may be waiting,
Right outside your bedroom'?

Ko Okuno (11)
Aberdour School

Petrified

It is red like the Devil.
It sounds like a lion roaring down your ear.
It smells like a rotten apple left in the sun.
It tastes like blood dripping down your throat.
It looks like a fire burning a baby.
It feels like a ghost sucking your flesh.
It reminds me of World War I.

James Bell (8)
Atwood Primary School

Happiness

It tastes like French bread freshly cooked in the oven.
It reminds me of me and my friends in the park getting sweets.
It smells like a cake being opened from a bakery.
It feels like a good feeling in my body.
It sounds like hip-hop music and rock music.
It looks like happy people and peace.

Liam Vickery (8)
Atwood Primary School

Excited

It is blue like the sky.
It reminds me of eating a baked pudding.
It smells like my mum saying she loves me.
It looks like my brain is about to explode with laughter.
It tastes like eating a cake.
It looks like having fun.
It sounds like R 'n' B music.

Harrison Weaver (8)
Atwood Primary School

Scared

It is black like spiders.
It smells like real aliens coming up the stairs.
It reminds me of pure black.
It looks like a zombie trying to get me.
It tastes like blood.
It feels like death coming to you.
It sounds like I am melting.

Jessica Callaghan (8)
Atwood Primary School

Angry

It is red like an open fire
It sounds like people fighting
It smells like a cloud of ash
It feels like a part of my head burning
It looks like lightning striking a tree
It tastes like chilli
It reminds me of when I want revenge.

Geoffrey Niu (9)
Atwood Primary School

Angry

It is red like a dreadful fire.
It feels like your finger snapping.
It smells like fish that have just come out of the water.
It looks like a cat bristling its fur.
It sounds like a person moaning.
It tastes like a snail crunching in your mouth.
It reminds me of spiders crawling everywhere.

Bekah King (8)
Atwood Primary School

Happiness

It is pink like my teddy
It looks like my friend Daniel
It smells like custard
It sounds like music
It feels like Milly, my dog
It tastes like chocolate cake.

Rachel Douglas (9)
Atwood Primary School

Frightened

It is black like an old grave
It tastes like 100-year-old chicken bones
It smells like human blood
It looks like a ghost saying, 'Boo!'
It feels like a mummy's tomb
It sounds like going to see a murder movie
It reminds me of going back to the Tudor times
                            and getting beheaded.

Gabriela Sachs (8)
Atwood Primary School

Excited

It smells like fresh air.
It's blue like the sky.
It reminds me of pencil cases banging on the tables.
It tastes like marshmallows in a sweet shop.
It feels like I'm going to burst.
It looks like a funny bunny right in front of me.
It sounds like a balloon going to *pop!*

Rosie Palmer (8)
Atwood Primary School

Delighted

It is blue like the sky shining
It sounds like birds singing
It smells like cakes baking
It tastes like lovely fresh air
It looks like nice people playing
It feels like holding something fluffy
It reminds me of glorious days.

Alexandria Bartolo (8)
Atwood Primary School

Scared

It is black like a dark room.
It tastes like a mouldy piece of liquorice.
It smells like the blood of death.
It sounds like a door creaking.
It looks like a pitch-black room.
It feels like you're inside out.
It reminds me of someone killing me.

Thomas Sutehall (9)
Atwood Primary School

Anger

It is red like a blush.
It tastes like a flame of boiling lava.
It smells like a rotten body.
It feels like an alien's guts.
It looks like a dead body.
It reminds me of running away from the world.
It sounds like the wind whistling with anger.

Mary Kelada (9)
Atwood Primary School

Bored

It is brown like the ground.
It sounds like rain pitter-pattering.
It smells like smoke all around.
It tastes like water.
It looks like grey clouds.
It feels like sitting alone.
It reminds me of Mondays!

Tom Combeer (8)
Atwood Primary School

Bored

It feels like old bricks lying in the middle of a field.
It tastes like mushy peas in a freezer.
It smells like someone has just been sick.
The colour is brown, like a fence.
It sounds like a clock ticking.
It reminds me of a boring brown cow.
It looks like a brown monkey.

Kerry Allen (8)
Atwood Primary School

Angry

It is red like a flame.
It sounds like people knocking down walls.
It smells like fresh leaves on a tree.
It tastes like someone sucking ink from a pen.
It looks like someone stomping around.
It feels like someone smacking something.
It reminds me of going to bed.

Jacob Rolfe (9)
Atwood Primary School

Scared

It is black like death.
It sounds like thunder.
It smells like horror.
It tastes like mud.
It looks like a ghost.
It feels like a spider crawling up your sleeve.
It reminds me of a sack.

Venous Kanuga (8)
Atwood Primary School

Terrified

It is red like blood
It sounds like thunder
It looks like blood from dead people
It smells like cold liver
It tastes like rotten cheese
It feels like deadly movies
It reminds me of going back in time to the Tudors
                                    and being beheaded.

Madelene Cowley (8)
Atwood Primary School

Excited

It's yellow, like a sunflower
It looks like a person who's happy
It tastes like ice cream
It smells like marshmallows melting in your mouth
It sounds like people laughing
It reminds me of having a party.

Stephanie Soosaipillai (8)
Atwood Primary School

Anger

It's red, like a red-hot frying pan.
It feels like the sun.
It sounds like those old kettles.
It tastes like chocolate drink.
It reminds me of red liquorice.
It looks like blood all over the place.
It smells of hot, boiled blood.
It smells of death.

John-Paul Black (8)
Atwood Primary School

Angry

It sounds like feet creeping up the stairs.
It feels like punching someone in the arm.
It sounds like a crowd of zombies coming to hurt my family.
It sounds like the same person who killed me.
It sounds like blood pumping round my body very fast.
It sounds like I'm in the dark forever.
It reminds me of yesterday.

Lauren Noone (9)
Atwood Primary School

Angry

It is black like the inside of my tummy.
It sounds like a chainsaw cutting wood.
It smells like a dungeon full of rats.
It tastes like a rotten apple.
It looks like glowing eyes.
It feels like a sharp nail.
It reminds me of a house burning down.

Bethany Reeve (8)
Atwood Primary School

The Rainy Day

The rain drops down on the window sill
Too wet to go outside
My rain mac has got a hole in it
The rain stops and I go outside
The puddles are huge
They go up to my knees
But then it starts to rain again
Oh dear, oh deary me.

Tom Broomfield (9)
Bushy Hill Junior School

Colours

What is blue?
The sea is blue, with dolphins jumping in and out

What is orange?
An orange is orange, with segments small but bright

What is pink?
A rose is pink, with its petals in full bloom

What is green?
The grass is green, swaying in the breeze

What is white?
The snow is white, crunching beneath our feet

What is red?
Blood is red, trickling through our bodies

What is silver?
A coin is silver, shining in the sun

What is black?
The night is black, darkening as we sleep

What is yellow?
The sun is yellow, glistening down to Earth

What is brown?
Dead leaves are brown, falling to the ground

What is colourful?
The whole world is colourful, brightening up our day.

Bradley Welch (8)
Bushy Hill Junior School

Cinderella

Poor Cinderella,
Sat alone,
Doing all the hard work,
Cooking and cleaning the home.

Never knew her mother,
Her dad was never there,
She lived in a mansion,
Her fridge was always bare.

She had two stepsisters,
Horrid and cruel
And their pet cat,
Who always drooled.

Anastasia and Drizzela
Were their names,
Causing misery for Cinderella,
Was their game.

Cinderella was invited to a ball,
But her stepsisters went instead,
It was in the palace hall,
So all Cinderella could do was lie in bed.

Her fairy godmother appeared,
With sparkles and glittery everywhere,
She said, 'Don't fear Cinderella,'
And soon fixed her make-up, dress and hair.

Cinderella ran to the palace,
Landed right in front of the prince,
He asked for a dance
And they were married in an instance.

Onika Khatun (10)
Bushy Hill Junior School

A Night In The Life Of A Vampire

A vampire gets up at night
When we all go to bed
The vampire puts on his cloak
For the fact that he is undead

He starts off by brushing his fangs
Until they shine and gleam
Then he gargles water
Straight from a polluted stream

A vampire sucks blood
Having a lot of fun
Until dawn comes
And out comes the sun

Then the vampire runs back to his coffin
Next he slams the door
To get a little bit of rest
For another dark night of bloodsucking galore.

Thomas Bailey (10)
Bushy Hill Junior School

Imagine

Imagine a flea as big as a bee,
Imagine a rat as fat as a cat,
Imagine a goat as wet as a boat.

Imagine a lion called Ryan,
Imagine an ape wearing a cape,
Imagine a snake wrapped round a rake,
Imagine a gorilla eating a chinchilla.

Imagine a squirrel, his nickname Terrel,
Imagine a camel eating a mammal,
Imagine a shark chewing on bark,
Imagine a dog eating a frog.

Suddenly, I woke up and my dream ended.

Charlotte Gallacher (11)
Bushy Hill Junior School

Water Is Great

(Inspired by Roger McGough's 'Trees are Great')

Water is great, it likes to shake,
It also likes to bake,
It's never tired, it keeps on moving,
Just like a little lake.

Water is great, it likes to eat cakes,
It's very tasty,
It's very nice,
It really likes the cold.

Water is great, it has no hates,
It comes from a cup,
It gives us hiccups,
I never knew that water was so good.

If we didn't have water,
What would we drink?
What would we cook with?
What would fish swim in?

Christopher Murray (7)
Bushy Hill Junior School

Rhyming Poem

Trees are tall
Trees are brown and green
Bees have yellow and black stripes
Bees make honey
Leaves can come in all different sizes
Leaves are red, green and brown
Peas are round
Peas are green
Queens have lots of jewels
Queens have a crown
Mean is when you are horrible
Clean is when you wash
Stop! No more!

Rosie Sandison (7)
Bushy Hill Junior School

The Number Party

Number one thought it such fun,
That number two got locked in the loo,
Number three needed a wee,
So number four knocked down the door,
Number five got buried alive,
So number six moved the bricks,
Number seven looked down from Heaven
And number eight pondered their fate,
Number nine said, 'What's the time?'
And number ten said, 'Not you again.'
Number one got out a gun,
So number two hid back in the loo,
Number three said, *I need a wee!*'
And number four said, 'No more, no more,'
Number five began to jive,
Cos number six played drums with sticks,
Number seven heard it from Heaven
And number eight thought, *this is great,*
But number nine did not think it fine,
That number ten said, 'Let's start again!'

Annie Sage (10)
Bushy Hill Junior School

Stretches

Got up this morning,
Stretched my arms and my bones,
Got up this morning,
Stretched my feet and my toes.

I stretch when I'm tired,
I stretch when I'm sleepy,
All of these stretches I do,
When I'm weepy.

George Cairns (10)
Bushy Hill Junior School

How Does A Spider Spin His Web?

How does a spider in his nineties spin his web?
He goes to the phone, picks it up,
He calls the Home Support Services and says,
'I'm an elderly spider and I can't spin my web,
I need to catch my dinner,
I am no longer a good spinner,
I like a good dinner of flies,
But I no longer have any supplies.'
The very next day along came a handy spider
Who said, 'I am a healthcare provider.'
He started to spin, spinning, spinning as he went,
The old spider's hunger he would prevent.
When it was finished, the spider said,
'Thanks for the web,'
Gave him a tip and went to bed in his brand new web.

Angus Dunnett (10)
Bushy Hill Junior School

Odd Socks

There's always one odd sock
So where do they go?
Does the washing machine eat them
Or swallow them whole?

Is there a monster inside it
Or do they just disappear?
Can they turn invisible
And can they reappear?

Could someone tell me where they go?
Cos just like you, I want to know.
Maybe we should hang them on a tree
To be reunited like a family.

Robyn Jankowski (10)
Bushy Hill Junior School

Fruit And Veg Alphabet

A is for apples, juicy and ripe
B is for banana, easy to bite
C is for carrot, tasty when boiled
D is for dates, growing on trees
E is for eggplant, shiny and black
F is for figs, growing on my grandma's tree
G is for grapes, succulent all round
H is for hoping for more
I is for interesting vegetables, sitting on my plate
J is for jam on my toast
K is for kiwi, green inside
L is for lettuce in my salad
M is for melon, shaped like a rugby ball
N is for nectarine, shaped like a juggling ball
O is for orange, bumpy all over
P is for pumpkin, carved at Hallowe'en
Q is for quince, smooth all round
R is for raspberry, sweet and lumpy
S is for smoothies, fruity and fine
T is for tasty, all fruit and veg
U is for united fruits all over the world
V is for vegetables, all different textures
W is for wacky, all sizes and shapes
X is for xylophone, played with all fruits
Y is for yellow, slapped on the lemon
Z is for zucchini in my pasta.

Anya Murdoch (7)
Bushy Hill Junior School

The Word Party!

(Inspired by 'The Word Party)

Angry words stamp and growl,
Shy words hide behind their towels,
Proud words give themselves a pat on the back,
Secret words have private gold sacks,
Ticklish words off their heads,
Tired words cuddle their teds,
Tall words crash their heads into trees,
Naughty words steal keys,
Funny words tell jokes,
Wet words get soaked,
Small words suck their thumbs,
Hard words do difficult sums,
Here comes . . .
Snap! The dictionary closes.

Maduri Satkunabalan (10)
Bushy Hill Junior School

My Dad

My dad cares
My dad shares
That's why I love him
My dad likes ice cream
My dad always works in a team
That's why I love him
My dad likes his tea
My dad likes me
That's why I love him so much.

Chanice Raynbird (9)
Bushy Hill Junior School

The Magic Garden

(Based on 'Magic Box' by Kit Wright)

I will put in the garden . . .

A smiling flower shimmering in the sun
A leaf of mint made into a blade of grass
A tree with all kinds of fruit

I will put in the garden . . .

The coldness of winter with a hot sun
The garden which talks to me
The trees that are made into buildings

I will put in the garden . . .

Birds that can fly backwards
Birds that speak your poems
Birds that have all the colours in the world

I will put in the garden . . .

Flowers that taste of candy
Flowers that look like people
Flowers that make you special

I will put in the garden . . .

A fruit that grows on grass
A fruit that lasts forever
A fruit that never loses its taste

I will put in the garden . . .

A cat that barks
A dog that miaows
A squirrel that eats leaves

I will put in the garden . . .

A blue sun
A pink moon
A purple cloud

I will put in the garden . . .

A patio that is squidgy
A pink table
A purple chair

I will put in the garden . . .

A pond full of blood
A stone made of clay
A crocodile that looks like a fish

I will put in the garden . . .

A tree trunk that is red
A branch that is orange
A patch of grass that is blue

Lucy Wolstencroft (8)
Bushy Hill Junior School

The Horse

I was standing on the gate, when I caught his eye,
Proud and strong and never shy,
He came towards me at such a pace,
I felt the warmth of the sun on my face.
His shadow was long, the sun was low,
Frost on the grass that had a glow,
Mane and tail flowing likes waves at sea,
Hooves hitting hard ground, he hastened to me.
With a snort and a whinny, he stopped at the gate,
My friend, the horse, always there, never late.

Rebecca McBean (10)
Bushy Hill Junior School

My Box

(Based on 'Magic Box' by Kit Wright)

I will put in my box . . .

A puppy that will soon be mine,
The angel on top of a Christmas tree,
Something from someone who is close to my heart.

I will put in my box . . .

The breeze on a summer's day,
A snowman with a smile on his face, somehow,
Coloured leaves falling from the trees in autumn.

I will put in my box something that nobody will ever know.

Georgia Bentham (8)
Bushy Hill Junior School

The Frog Hop

Frogs over here,
Frogs over there,
Frogs appearing everywhere.

Jumping high,
Leaping low,
Going with the river's flow.

Frogs saying ribbit,
Sometimes it sounds like leave it,
So many frogs that I love to hear.

Sam Dean (8)
Bushy Hill Junior School

Hate

Hate is black, like crashing thunder
It sounds like bombs raining down
It tastes like squeezing lemons into your mouth
It smells of burning petrol and oil
It feels hard and sharp, like a line of razor blades
It reminds me of my mum and dad watching the news.

Daniel Cogswell (9)
Greenvale Primary School

Fear

It sounds like the sirens on a police car.
It tastes like eating pigs' eyeballs.
It smells like rotting sewage.
It feels like the pain when bleeding to death.
It reminds me of my mum shouting.

Louis Hayes (9)
Greenvale Primary School

Animal World

Tiger, shark, lion, whale,
Some of the animals of the animal world.
Butterfly, dragonfly, mayfly, flutter by.
Leopard, cheetah and jaguar, predators from afar.
Chimpanzee and me, a happy family.
I like this, we like that,
Me and my animals, just me and my animals.

Jessica Newcombe (8)
Greenvale Primary School

Love

Love is like red, romantic roses
It sounds like the music of Barry White and Rhianna singing
It tastes like chocolates and red and white wine sparkling
It smells like red, red roses and bubbling champagne
It feels like a romantic valentine's card sent to you in a red envelope
It reminds me of the family, that I love.

Sophia Hinkley (9)
Greenvale Primary School

Love

Love is pink and red, like a beautiful bouquet of flowers,
Love is two little birds singing love songs early in the morning,
Love is sweet lovely chocolate cake, like love cake,
Love is a soft, white, blue-eyed cat purring contentedly on my pillow,
Love is the bond I feel when I hold a baby rabbit from the pet shop.

Caroline Francis (9)
Greenvale Primary School

Love

Love is red, like a human heart.
It sounds like two little birds singing.
It tastes like a big box of chocolates.
It smells like pretty perfume.
It reminds me of spring and roses.

Rebecca Thompson (9)
Greenvale Primary School

Happiness

Happiness is orange, like all your friends playing together.
It sounds like bubbly voices put together.
It tastes like a box of creamy chocolates.
It smells like melted caramel.
It feels like a cute, fluffy teddy bear.
It reminds me of my friends.

Nikhita Sharma (9)
Greenvale Primary School

Love

It sounds like birds singing sweet music,
It tastes like running chocolate on a waterfall,
It looks like happy roses in the sun,
It feels like polar bears in the hot summer's sun,
It smells like happy butterflies prancing with their friends,
It reminds me of my family.

Bethany Mills (9)
Greenvale Primary School

Anger

Anger is red, like bubbling lava
It sounds like an erupting volcano
It tastes like a fizzy sherbet sweet that has left my tongue numb
It smells like burning rubber
It feels like an angry bull charging at you
It reminds me of the day I was banned from the computer.

Max Smith (9)
Greenvale Primary School

Love

Love is red and pink, like a fresh bunch of pretty roses from my
mum's shop,
Love sounds like birds singing merrily in the morning when I wake up,
Love tastes like a lovely box of chocolates ready to eat,
Love smells like lovely cakes cooking in the oven, nearly ready
to eat,
Love feels like the teddy bear called Angel who I love to cuddle,
Love reminds me of spending time with my family.

Emily Tann (9)
Greenvale Primary School

Hate

Hate is red, like seeing spitting fire burning a rainforest, wrecking
homes of small animals.
It sounds like the scream of innocent people when a bomb goes off.
It tastes like 20 red-hot chilli peppers burning my mouth.
It smells like burning wood at the bottom of a bonfire.
It feels like a dagger plunging into my stomach.
It reminds me of lightning striking in a storm.

Akash Harnal (9)
Greenvale Primary School

Happiness

Happiness is yellow, like the sun
It sounds like laughter of children playing
It tastes like chocolate melting in my mouth
It feels like a warm cuddle from my family
It smells like freshly cut grass
It reminds me of going on holiday with my family.

Sophie Langworthy (9)
Greenvale Primary School

Hate

Hate is as red as fire burning out of control.
It sounds like nails scratching on a blackboard.
It tastes like rotten warm eggs.
It smells like out-of-date milk with mould.
It feels like getting punched in the guts.
It reminds me of the look on my mum's face when I won't
stop talking.

Emily Lloyd (9)
Greenvale Primary School

Love

Love feels like lying on a cotton wool bed sound asleep.
Love tastes like the softest candyfloss melting in your mouth.
Love sounds like the sweetest album of Tom Jones.
Love looks like a beautiful bunch of flowers.
Love smells like a big bowl of pot pourri.
Love is the colour red, like strawberries, pink like a bunch of tulips
and white like a bride's dress.

Katie Standen (9)
Greenvale Primary School

Anger

Anger is red, like a flaring fire in a mansion.
It sounds like nails scraping down a blackboard.
It smells like the stench of a threatened skunk.
It tastes like out of date and sour rhubarb.
It feels like a rock, as sharp as a meat cleaver.
It reminds me of the wrath of a splurting volcano.

Stefan Amokwandoh (10)
Greenvale Primary School

Love

Love is the colour of a red rose blossoming every spring,
It tastes like the fresh, warm, humid air flowing all around me,
It looks like the shimmering sun setting, ready to be night,
It feels like your soft, comfy bed, ready for you to snuggle up in,
It sounds like little birds singing beautifully whilst they flap their
                                                          tiny wings,
It reminds me of my caring, kind, loving family.

Katja Morris (9)
Greenvale Primary School

Love

Love is the colour of pale pinks and reds, like glimmering hearts.
It feels like a flowing river and the shining stars.
It sounds like birds singing sweetly in the fresh air.
Love looks like fresh roses in a plain bed of grass.
Love tastes like swirling butterflies beautifully dancing in the sun.
It smells like creamy chocolates waiting to be eaten.

Victoria Brennan (9)
Greenvale Primary School

The Moon

The moon is a bright and shining star,
When you look out the window, you see it from afar.
It is a light to keep you safe at night
And all the children in its sight.

Lauren El-Bishlawi & Elle Westcott (8)
Greenvale Primary School

Hate

It sounds like the Twin Towers collapsing.
It tastes like rotten apples.
It reminds me of World War II.
It smells like car fumes.
It feels like fire in my eyes.
It looks like countries at war.
Its colour is black.

Mitchell Farrington (9)
Greenvale Primary School

Happiness

Happiness is yellow, like sweet lemon slices in my mouth
It sounds like a bell tinkling in my ear
It is sweet and sour like a lime
It smells like sweet chocolate melting in front of my eyes.

Liam Jones (10)
Greenvale Primary School

Children Of The Week

Monday's child can win a race
Tuesday's child can pull a face
Wednesday's child enjoys her food
Thursday's child is very rude
Friday's child likes to sew
Saturday's child wears a bow
But the child that is born on the seventh day
Is loving and giving and enjoys their singing.

Helena Dawes (9)
St Catherine's Preparatory School, Guildford

Look At Me

Look at me
With ears to hear
A nose to smell
And eyes to see
Look at me.

Look at me
With hair to grow
A mouth to speak
And teeth to eat
Look at me.

Look at me
With shoulders to shrug
And fingers to touch
On hands that hold
Look at me.

Look at me
With legs to walk
Knees to bend
And feet to tread
Look at me.

Look at us
With the birds that fly
And the fish that swim
What a miracle
Look at me.

Megan Flint (9)
St Catherine's Preparatory School, Guildford

Peter And His Arms

There once was a young man called Peter
Whose arms were as long as ten metres!
They may have been long
But they weren't very strong
As he could not lift even one litre!

Georgia Leverett (10)
St Catherine's Preparatory School, Guildford

Ode To A Sink

Oh sink, you are my passion,
You're wonderful
And I'll cherish you.
Your gurgle trickles to my heart,
I love you,
I cherish you
And I believe in you.
You float past me in my sleep,
Whenever I glare at you,
You seem to come alive.
I devote my love to you,
You are my king and my queen,
Your taps glow and that reaches my love
And at night the silver moon shines down on you.
Your trickling drip of the taps is divine to my ears,
I'm not washing in the shower
Or the bath,
Only in you, my sink!

Ellie Backhouse (9)
St Catherine's Preparatory School, Guildford

Who Am I?

I come in many different colours
Pink, red, black and white
Most people like me
So do most bugs
I have a long green stem
With prickly leaves
That hurt when you try to pick me
When I am red, I am a love sign
When I am white, brides sometimes carry me
When I am black, I become rare
But when I am pink, I am common.
Who am I?

Faith Browning (9)
St Catherine's Preparatory School, Guildford

My Feelings About The Seasons

When I got up on the first of January
And heard the robin sing
My heart lifted up just like the sun
I felt like I had wings

On the first of April
The daffodils were formed
Tulips sprang high above the ground
As soon as I saw these wonderful flowers
I felt utterly warmed

On the first of July it was baking hot
Someone told me you could fry an egg on your head
It was a relief to get in the swimming pool
And get to go later to bed

On the first of October
I heard the wind calling me
I got changed and ran to the bottom of the garden
I saw a blanket of leaves all swaying merrily

When I got up on the first of December
There were only a few days to go
Santa Claus would come and visit soon
But don't open the presents yet, oh no!

Every month has different weather
I love the moods it wakes in me
Now I have explained all sorts of seasons
And they pass us by for you to see.

Ellen Dixon (9)
St Catherine's Preparatory School, Guildford

The Tiger

A sun-bright coat
And black, silken lines,
Eyes shining like blue moons,
Penetrating the darkness,
With a piercing gaze.

Lying in wait to pounce on his prey,
But not going too well so far,
All he can spy is a golden sea.
But no, he has spied
A wildebeest in the distance.

If you hear the *thunk, thunk, thunk*
Of pounding paws,
Stay out of the way,
For the tiger is coming . . .
To dinner!

Charlotte Owens (10)
St Catherine's Preparatory School, Guildford

Henry VIII

Henry VIII
Was big and great
He loved all the foods
That were put on his plate.
Henry VIII loved the Pope
Then one day
He hated the bloke.
He had six wives
Who mostly told lies
And didn't enjoy
His huge apple pies.

Megan Lucas (9)
St Catherine's Preparatory School, Guildford

Looking Inside My Marble

Inside my marble I can see coloured patterns going round and round
Inside my marble I can see swirls
Inside my marble I can see glittery flowers
Inside my marble I can see people everywhere
Inside my marble I can see bright stars
Inside my marble I can see a beautiful sunset

I would love to go inside my marble!

Arabella Pearson (9)
St Catherine's Preparatory School, Guildford

My Nightmare Journey

Our nightmare began when we drove in our car
From Guildford to Bath and we hadn't got far.
We were going quite fast on the busy M4
When the car made a beep and wouldn't go anymore.

The engine went bang, there was lots of black smoke
My brother was sleeping so I gave him a poke.
We jumped out of the car and sat by the road
And were asking ourselves if we'd have to be towed.

We ate popcorn and cake 'til the breakdown man came
My mum and my dad gave the garage the blame.
The RAC came with a toolbox and van
He waved to me and I thought, *what a nice man.*

Half an hour later we were back on our way
But that wasn't the end, I'm sorry to say.
We broke down again and another time too
And the traffic behind us was starting to queue.

The police came along and stopped right behind us
And suggested we parked and got on a bus.
But once they had gone, we got back on track
And with a couple more stops, we finally got back.

Christy Palmer (10)
St Catherine's Preparatory School, Guildford

Worm

Worm, worm, squiggle and squirm
In the soil you roam
Worm, worm, squiggle and squirm
What a squalid place is home.

Your skin is slimy
And your eyes are red
In and out of mud
Up pops your head.

Worm, worm, squiggle and squirm
In the soil you roam
Worm, worm, squiggle and squirm
What a squalid place is home.

You slither like a snake
And wriggle through the grass
You have no arms or legs
I see you as I pass.

Worm, worm, squiggle and squirm
In the soil you roam
Worm, worm, squiggle and squirm
What a squalid place is home.

Chloe Carruthers (10)
St Catherine's Preparatory School, Guildford

The Arctic Fox

White as the snow in the winter,
As he silently prowls the snow-covered wood,
As soon as his prey has been seen,
Like a shot, the animal's got.

The agility of the Arctic fox's pounce,
As he moves like a thunderbolt,
As soon as some prey has been seen,
Like a shot, the animal's got.

Ciara Milligan (10)
St Catherine's Preparatory School, Guildford

The Sea

I lived by the sea from the age of three
I watched the motion of this beautiful ocean
From my balcony

It was peaceful and quiet
Serene and silent
On the calm sea

When clouds were whirling and the sea was swirling
The ocean turned from azure to green
It was the most incredible scene

When the sea hits the rocks
The foam's white as socks
Splishing and splashing, in rock pools it crashes

With the setting of the sun
When the boats go out gliding
Gentle lapping of the shore means the day is no more.

Freya MacAngus (10)
St Catherine's Preparatory School, Guildford

Materials

There's silk
There's cotton
But I love fluff
It is cuddly
It is cosy
I love it!
There's velvet
There's wool
But I love lace
It is beautiful
It is smart
I love it!

Annabelle Body (9)
St Catherine's Preparatory School, Guildford

I Wish . . .

I wish I were a film star
I'd dominate TV
Every time you turned it on
All you'd see was me

I wish I were a model
Queen of every shot
Prancing down the catwalk
Wearing Gucci boots

I wish I were a pop star
With CDs in the shops
Everyone would love me
The great princess of pop

I wish I were an actress
Signing autographs
I'd leap about the West End stage
Making people laugh

Singing down my hairbrush
To my rubber duck
Dancing up the staircase
All I need is luck.

Catriona May (10)
St Catherine's Preparatory School, Guildford

Teachers

Teachers can be tricky
But can certainly be witty
The best one anyone can find
Is funny, firm and always kind

So if you want to find a teach
They are there within your reach
Around the corner, on a bus
So don't go making such a fuss.

Natasha Allan (10)
St Catherine's Preparatory School, Guildford

The Race

The race was the best thing I've ever seen
But some of the riders were pretty mean
They rode strange creatures that were very fast
I thought that none of them would come last.

One of the creatures was spiky and hairy
One of them looked just like a fairy!
But the beast that I liked the most
Was a giant lizard, his rider like a ghost

The green light went off at the starting line
I was worried about the ghost, his beast so fine
But to my amazement, with so much power
The lizard went off at 200 miles an hour!

Suddenly, the race ended
The rider had won, so my worries were mended
I looked at the beast, he was gold and black
Then he winked at me, so I winked back.

Danielle Smith-Suarez (10)
St Catherine's Preparatory School, Guildford

Football Fever!

Rooney nervous, feeling funny
Terry saying, 'Come on boys, hurry'
Gerrard squeezing the child's hand
Lampard putting on his sweatband
The manager eagerly waiting for it to begin.

Proudly the players stride onto the pitch
The game begins without a hitch
The sound of the fans becomes a roar
Rooney dribbles, shoots and scores!
In my dream the World Cup is England's once more.

Ellie Pilkington (10)
St Catherine's Preparatory School, Guildford

I Wish I Were Away In Wonderland

Oh, I wish I were away in wonderland,
With flowers blue and red,
The trees would wave and smile at me,
And never shake their heads.

Oh, I wish I were away in wonderland,
With houses made of wood,
No taxis, buses and pollution,
To ruin what has stood.

Oh, I wish I were away in wonderland,
With Mummy, Daddy and Sophie,
We'd live in a little cottage,
With a little doggy called Daisy.

Oh, I wish I were away in wonderland,
But instead I live in London,
In a block of big red flats
And also there's the dungeon!

Abigail Ashby (11)
St Catherine's Preparatory School, Guildford

I Love My Mummy

I love my mummy
She's very funny
She tells some very good jokes.

I love my mummy
I came from her tummy
She made me with all her love.

I love my mummy
She's very yummy
And a pretty good cook as well.

I love my mummy
(You might have already guessed that)
And she's the best mummy in the world!

Maisie La Costa (10)
St Catherine's Preparatory School, Guildford

A Taste Of Autumn

Taste autumn in the woods,
When the leaves turn golden
And crunch beneath your feet.

Taste autumn in the sky,
When the birds migrate
And fly south.

Taste autumn in the orchard,
Where the apples and pears are ripening
And getting ready to eat.

Taste autumn in the wind,
When conkers fall
And children play their games.

Taste autumn in the evenings,
When the days get shorter
And the air is crisp.

Georgina Steele (10)
St Catherine's Preparatory School, Guildford

Friends

I have lots of friends,
Some are tall and some are small,
Some like different things,
From Pokémon to style and back again!

I don't have any best friends, but lots of friends,
We like each other and play with each other,
Just like friends should be.

I think that all of my friends have different qualities of me,
Like the God of Hinduism,
One of my friends loves to draw, so we do that together
And another one loves tennis, so we do that together.

I think that my friends are part of what makes me, me!

Grace Richardson (11)
St Catherine's Preparatory School, Guildford

Sport

Sport, sport, I love sport
It is fun
It is great
It keeps you strong and fit

Sport, sport, I love sport
There are lots of sports to play
You can do one every day
They are fun to play

Sport, sport, I love sport
Some you kick
Some you throw
And some you use a stick

Sport, sport, I love sport
You can play with your friends
And in gymnastics you do lots of bends
I like sport the best.

Megan Cowx (11)
St Catherine's Preparatory School, Guildford

The Green Woodpecker

Oh! my feathered, handsome friend
With a cloak of red and a crown of green.
Many insects meet their end
By your sharp, fierce beak and eyes so keen.

What's that under the tree bark?
Hear a noise? There is it again . . . *lick!*
Insects flee the jaws so dark.
It's too late, he's snatched them up quick!

Today's meal now finished he
Takes to the sky, sharp talons at ease.
Home to his mate in her tree?
Watch his wings gracefully rest on the breeze.

Anna Lucas-Clements (10)
St Catherine's Preparatory School, Guildford

The Three Witches

One cold and frosty night,
Three witches stood in the moonlight.
They cackled and rattled,
They yelled and battled,
Over a piping hot cauldron.

'We'll cast a spell,
We'll make it smell,
We'll bubble and bubble and bake it,
But first we'll add some rats and bats,
To make the spell complete.

Bubble, bubble, toil and trouble,
Cast a spell and make it double.
Eye of rabbit, eye of sheep,
Mix it together, which makes you sleep.
Bubble, bubble, toil and trouble,
Cast a spell and make it double.
Racoon's tail and howlet's wing,
Mix them together, which makes you sing.
Bubble, bubble, toil and trouble,
Cast a spell and make it double.
Lizard's leg and adder's fork,
Mix together, which makes you talk.
Bubble, bubble, toil and trouble,
Cast a spell and make it double.'

Ellen Bryden (10)
St Catherine's Preparatory School, Guildford

Winter Is Here

Winter is when the weather is
Cold and roads are icy

Winter is when Jack Frost
Comes to visit you at night

Winter is when thick snow
Hits the icy, stiff grass

Winter is when children
Build their snowmen

Winter is when ponds freeze
Over and are perfect for ice skating

Winter is when the witches
Fly in the sky on Hallowe'en

Winter is when you gather around
The fire to melt marshmallows

Winter is when colourful fireworks
Light up the sky on Bonfire Night

Winter is when Christmas comes
And Santa delivers our presents

Winter is over when spring arrives
And everything starts to grow again.

Lucy Barker-Hahlo (10)
St Catherine's Preparatory School, Guildford

Poem Of Colours

Orange is the colour of sunrise,
Blended with a hint of yellow,
All is calm and peaceful,
All is gentle and mellow.

Light blue is the colour of the sky,
Where the eagles eye their prey,
Blue tits feed their young,
It is the beginning of a new day.

Yellow is the colour of the sun,
It brightens up the day,
And all the children come outside,
To sing and dance and play.

Dark blue is the colour of the sea,
Where fishes love to roam,
The waves keep crashing onwards,
Creating streaks of foam.

Pink is the colour of the sunset,
Added with orange and green,
It is a beautiful sight to see,
Sometimes you see it in your dreams.

Black is the colour of night,
Where bats echo in caves,
And when the moon comes out,
It changes its phase.

Nothing is the colour of sleep,
Except the colours of your dreams,
Which take you on a journey,
Nothing is what it seems.

Emily Fairweather (10)
St Catherine's Preparatory School, Guildford

When You're Over The Moon

When you're over the moon,
You see sparkling stars in silvery light
And you dream of purple mountains,
When in bed tucked up tight.

Fluffy white clouds are drifting above,
In the baby-blue sky,
You can smell roses and daisies,
Hanging on moonbeams up high.

You feel so happy,
So full of joy,
You want a big hug,
From a cuddly toy.

Beaming sunshine,
Beautiful flowers,
You could be out in the buttercups,
For hours and hours.

I'm so over the moon,
I could grow wings
And flutter like a butterfly,
Or the bluebird that sings.

Lots of smiles,
Happy laughter,
You feel so great
And will be forever after.

Megan von Spreckelsen (10)
St Catherine's Preparatory School, Guildford

A Drop Of Water

I start in the sky,
As a big puffy cloud
I then start to rain, sometimes very loud.
I meander down the river,
Like a snake having a slither.

I am rather small,
But sometimes I stand out tall,
When the people in Africa need me to survive.
I flow into the sea,
Where all the fish swim past me.
The steaming hot sun begins to flare,
Then I evaporate into thin air.

I rise higher and higher until I feel cold,
I then go through condensation or so I am told.
I form a cloud and the wind carries me away.
I then hover in the sky waiting to rain,
Once more the tiring cycle starts again.

Libby Jeffery (10)
St Catherine's Preparatory School, Guildford

Newspaper

In newspapers now you see such tiresome things,
Like stocks and shares drop, undercooked chicken wings,
Tony Blair's out, new prime minister elected,
Flood in Cranleigh, robbery detected.

I'd much prefer to hear things like,
Ginny Davis has lost her bike,
The tale of the fearless flea-ridden cat
And *very* important stuff like that.

But Mum says it's drivel, Dad says it's a mess,
But I find it better than their daily press.

Helen Goldsbrough (10)
St Catherine's Preparatory School, Guildford

The Roller-Coaster Ride

It looked scary,
I was very wary.
I got on,
Next to my friend John.
It set off with a jolt,
I hope it's not a fault.
The other rides were near,
As we whizzed by with fear.
It was bumpy
And very jumpy.
It went this way and that,
As I held on to my hat.
It spun,
As I started to have fun.
It had nearly stopped
And soon off we hopped.

Victoria Schenk (10)
St Catherine's Preparatory School, Guildford

Crabbing In Seaview

Over the sands to Priory Bay
The crabs and lobsters make their way
Into the water green and cool
Diving into their favourite pool.

I wander on when the tide is low
With nets and buckets all in tow
Hoping and wishing it will be the night
When I get a really big bite.

Crouching low I dip my net
So far down my arm got wet
Here he is, an enormous crab
I jump for joy and feel so glad.

Another happy day by the sea
Seaview is the place for me.

Milly Smith (10)
St Catherine's Preparatory School, Guildford

Game, Set And Match

Months of practise
Hitting balls
Perfecting my shots
Making calls.

Step up to the line
Ready to serve
I'd love an ace
Need to hold my nerve.

Forehand cross court
Return down the line
Run in to volley
The point is mine.

Another long rally
She's in at the net
Hit my high lob
Yes! I've won the set.

I have a match point
And tension is high
I hit a great winner
Raise my arms to the sky.

Lottie Palmer (10)
St Catherine's Preparatory School, Guildford

Mystery

Mystery,
What is here in this wood?
Is there more than the gentle, burbling stream?
More than the rotting trees?
Yes.
There are the flickering lights,
That grow larger at night,
There are the strange whispers that I hear,
Yes, there is mystery here.

Mystery,
What are the whispers?
Who whispers stories in my ear?
Sends pictures in my head?
I know.
They are the trees,
They are their stories,
They are their songs,
Yes, there is mystery here.

Mystery,
How do they do it?
Why do they do it?
Because
I'm special,
I'm strange,
Yes, I am mystery.

Lucy Courage (10)
St Catherine's Preparatory School, Guildford

Maple Stud

Driving down the lane to the stables
I look out of the window and see,
A newborn foal, a pony and horses
And it all amazes me.

Through the gate to where we park,
I clamber out and gather my gear,
I see my horse in the yard, it's huge,
And my tummy flips over in fear.

Katie shouts that I am late again,
That I have nearly run out of time,
Hat firmly on, I rush to the block
And once up, I know that I'm fine.

In the ring we walk, trot and canter,
The time flies by, I'm having such fun.
Soon Katie's opening the gate to finish
And the smile on her face says well done.

Roseanna Windsor-Lewis (10)
St Catherine's Preparatory School, Guildford

Mystery?

In the black of the night,
You can hardly see this magical sight.
It beats its wings in a slow, pounding rhythm,
This mighty beast is the King of Evil.

Fangs gleam, eyes stare,
Powerful jaws with large, toothpick teeth.
Squinting through the clouds he seeks his prey,
Five humans is a feast.

He snacks on cows and sheep,
Humans look out, you're its prey.
Kill it must do,
And eat you.

Though it's just a myth,
Just believe this;
You may be next
To see the Devil's chest.

Madelaine Salvage (10)
St Catherine's Preparatory School, Guildford

The Waterfall, Lake And Fish

The sparkling stream fell quickly down the waterfall,
As it fell, it dripped into the lake where all the fish lived.
The tingly sound of the water made me all curious inside.

The huge lake with all the lilies on it,
Filled with fish of all sorts.
When a bit of bread tumbled into the lake,
All the fish rushed up to the surface.
That's the life in the water.

Now the waterfall is trickling in the summer sun,
The lake with lilies upon the surface glistening gold,
Moved when the fish swam.
The quick flashes of bullion underneath the surface,
Make me startle.
I love the water.

Katie Hillan (11)
St Catherine's Preparatory School, Guildford

The Magical House

Come on, come on into the magical house,
Come on, come on to see the magical mouse,
It can whizz you right away,
So you can spend a magical day.
It will whoosh you up so high,
Till you'll surely reach the sky,
There you'll have some blueberry pie,
Then you'll turn into a magical fly.

Come on, come on into the magical house,
Come on, come on to see the magical mouse,
There are magical colours, red and green,
The most amazing you've ever seen.
The code is 5, 2, 1 and 4,
Which will take you through the magical door,
Please do pop along very soon,
It is open every day at noon.

Jordan Glass (10)
St Peter's Primary School, South Croydon

Things I Do

I hate flies
But I love pies.

I am very glam
But I hate sham.

I love my dad
But he can be mad.

I love my mum
But she can be a plum.

I love to go in the car
Very, very far.

I love school
It's better than being a fool.

I love to chat
With my cat.

These are the things I do
What about you?

Maryam Haque (10)
St Peter's Primary School, South Croydon

My Cat

I'm going to tell you about my cat
She's ginger and white and very fat
Her name is Charlie and she's nine years old
She's a cuddly coward who's never been bold.

When we're out in the garden
We have so much fun
You should see her belly wobble
When she tries to run.

I love to stroke her ginger fur
And when I do she starts to purr
I love the way her fur is ginger
When she stalks a bird, she's like a ninja.

Arrun Hawkins (10)
St Peter's Primary School, South Croydon

Your Heart

If you are not sure
Which way to go . . .

Ask your heart
Your heart will know.

When your mind
Does not know what to say . . .

Your heart will
Find a way.

When you can't see
The finishing line

Or when your dreams
Seem hard to find . . .

Know that you know the way
Your heart will lead you there one day.

Amber Smith (10)
St Peter's Primary School, South Croydon

Animals In My Life

I like dogs and I like cats,
Hamsters are OK, but not big rats.
In the zoo we see the cheetah
And the gorilla, what a big eater!
The tortoises are slow, the tigers are quick,
The snakes are slithery and very slick.
The parrots are noisy, the turtles are quiet,
Not like the chimps, who cause a big riot.
But my favourite of all is very, very tall,
He eats leaves off trees and doesn't like fleas.
It's a giraffe!

Ceilidh Harris (10)
St Peter's Primary School, South Croydon

Who Is In Your Family?

She's pretty, she's fun, she's great,
She puts yummy food on my plate,
Who is she? My mum.

He's mad, he's bad, he's the best one I've ever had,
He makes me laugh and smile,
Who, you ask? My dad!

His glasses slip off the end of his nose,
As he drifts off for a doze.
When he's in his chair he looks like a fluffy bear.
Who is he? My grandad.

She always loses her keys or her bag,
She always has a good nag,
She likes little cats but doesn't like rats.
Who? My gran!

He has pointy ears and a little wet nose,
Sharp claws on the end of his toes.
He is my cat!

Fenella Matlock (11)
St Peter's Primary School, South Croydon

My Annoying Little Sister

I tried to hit my little sister,
But I didn't 'cause I missed her.
But then my twister of a sister took a bat
And whacked me like that on a certain spot,
Which hurt me quite a lot,
'Cause the bit she did hit was hurting where I sat.

As I rolled in pain I cried, 'I'm going to get you!'
But she mockingly replied, 'Did I upset you?
Well, that's a shame and it serves you right
And the next time you pick a fight,
Don't try it 'cause you might be knocked out.
Right!'

Bethany Baden (10)
St Peter's Primary School, South Croydon

My Pets

I have loads of pets
And they always make sounds like jumbo jets.
They love the colour blue,
But they never seem to come up to you.
I like them the most,
But they always snuggle up with a lamp post.
They don't like sweets,
But they do like treats.
They are so nice,
But they like the word ice.
They are always weird,
But now they have disappeared.
I've got to find them,
Now one of them picked up a pen.
They don't like flea powder,
But they do like flowers.
I don't know why,
Perhaps one day one of them will swallow a fly.

Grace Audus (7)
St Peter's Primary School, South Croydon

Shark

The shark circles around its prey,
It lives underwater all night and day.

The shark attacks without a sound,
You'll see him going round and round.

When he is there, you can't see him,
All you can see is a big pointy fin.

All you can see is a splash in the water,
You can rely on the shark that caught her.

Ryan Sibbald (10)
St Peter's Primary School, South Croydon

I Saw A Mouse

I saw a mouse
Running around in my bungalow
I shouted, 'Hey!'
But it sped away
And I didn't see it anymore.

I saw a mouse, a tiny mouse
Running around my house
I cried out, 'Hi!'
But it was so shy
It left without saying goodbye.

I saw a mouse in my flat
Running in the corridor
I said, 'Hello!'
Showed him my cat
But I think he was too scared of that.

I saw a mouse in my room
I offered it some soup from my spoon
But he took offence
And became so tense
That he jumped out of the window
Right into the fence.

Hope Bryan (7)
St Peter's Primary School, South Croydon

Football

The ball is the game's key
He gets the ball and gives it to me
I trap the ball with my sole
And shoot the ball and score a goal.

We have to start to pull up our socks
And get the ball in the eighteen yard box
We have to play the way our tactics are set
To get the ball in the back of the net.

Zubair Amin (11)
St Peter's Primary School, South Croydon

I'm Dead!

One day I stepped out of bed
And saw that I was dead.
'Oh, gracious me,' I said
As I looked straight through my head.
How will I tell my mum?
I bet she'll look quite glum.
Oh, I'm being very dumb,
Although I do feel very numb.
How could I have expired?
I bet I will be fired
And I will not be admired.
I'm starting to feel tired,
I'd better go to Heaven,
The gates close at eleven,
Phew, it's only seven!
I wonder if God's called Kevin?
To get in it's £1.97.

Madeleine Wilson (10)
St Peter's Primary School, South Croydon

First Day Of School

I walk through the gates
And what I see,
Is something completely new to me.
We have things called lessons,
Like ICT,
My favourite though has to be PE.
We write with pencils
And colour with pens,
The only table I've learnt though are the tens.
I'm here for years
And I've got a lot to do,
I've been here a month and I'm still called new!

Lydia Hunter (9)
St Peter's Primary School, South Croydon

Young Writers - A Pocketful Of Rhyme Verses From Surrey

The Kind School

I go through the door
And everyone stares at me
I see new people
I make new friends
I like all the lessons
I'm very good at PE
I look behind me
And then I see
Someone I know
And then I say, 'I know you.'
She says back to me, 'I know you too.'
I look around the loo
And they are very new
When I'm in class
I see my new teacher
She smiles at you
She smiles at other people too
This is the end of my first day of school.

Reece Bage (9)
St Peter's Primary School, South Croydon

The Annoying Thing

When something bugs you
You get really mad
But don't stop, carry on
Take it out on yourself
Because nobody gets hurt then
Everyone likes doing something
If you're playing football
And you miss a penalty
Don't worry
Most of the England team can't score.

Joshua Mullins (9)
St Peter's Primary School, South Croydon

Play With Me

Play with me,
Play with me,
I'm really nice,
I may be quiet, just like mice,
But I'm as friendly as can be.
Why doesn't anyone play with me?
Please come to my house,
We can play football,
I will just lean on the wall,
If no one plays with me.
I haven't smiled since last week
Because no one looks or cares about me.
'Can I play football with you?'
The boy nodded and said, 'Yes.'
I've just kicked the ball into the goal!
Everyone is playing with me,
I'm as happy as can be.

Joshua Anderson (7)
St Peter's Primary School, South Croydon

No!

'Can I go to the toilet Miss?'
'No!'
'Can I go and boil it Miss?'
'No!'
'Can I dig up the soil Miss?'
'No!'
'Can we go outside Miss?'
'No!'
'Can we go home Miss? What do you think?'
'Yes child go home, I want to be in peace.'

Anna Maria Loizou (10)
St Peter's Primary School, South Croydon

Christmas Poem

C hristmas lights and lots of snow
H owling wind in the trees
R unning children in the breeze
I cy windows, icy leaves
S ledging down the mountains green
T omorrow will be so much fun making friends with everyone
M um's cooking Christmas lunch
A s the reindeer fly up high
S anta sleighing right behind them.

Charley Turner (9)
St Peter's Primary School, South Croydon

A Harvest Poem

H arvest food here and there
A utumn leaves falling down
R abbits hopping everywhere
V ery cold at night
E verywhere red, yellow and brown crunchy leaves on the ground
S team engines' smoke, misty in the air
T he end of harvest, food here and there.

Leah Clifton-Dey (10)
St Peter's Primary School, South Croydon

My Mum

My mum's fun and she plays the drums swiftly.
My mum's cool and she really is tall.
My mum's very funny, like a bouncy Easter bunny.
My mum's super rich and she likes to stitch.
My mum's really neat and she likes to eat all the meat.
My mum's clever and she looks up to Heaven.

Maggie May (9)
St Peter's Primary School, South Croydon

The Apple Tree

One stormy day I saw an apple tree,
I grabbed an apple and it spoke to me:
'I'll grant you a wish if you let me free,'
So I threw it back into the apple tree.

Today I picked up that apple under the tree,
I stood still and it spoke to me:
'I'll grant you a wish if you let me free,'
So I thought about chucking it back in the tree . . .

It was delicious and nutritious . . . *crunch!*

Kade Stroude (9)
St Peter's Primary School, South Croydon

Sonic

Sonic is the fastest,
The fastest in the land,
He can go faster,
Than the amazing speed of sound.

He made a sonic *boom,*
He heard his friend called Tails
And hoped he'd see him soon,
Then he got bored and went into the zoo!

Dean Chalk (9)
St Peter's Primary School, South Croydon

My Cat

My cat is so sleepy,
You wouldn't know until it's time to be fed.
It goes under the table,
Miaowing very loudly
For all to hear.
For food in her tummy,

Amy Jones (9)
St Peter's Primary School, South Croydon

The Star Wars Poem

S tar Wars has lots of battles
T he planets have lots of weird aliens
A nd the spaceships are enormous and speedy
R unning creatures weird and wacky

W reckage from past battles
A mazing characters
R 2-D2 squealing loudly
S tar Wars is a brilliant film!

Thomas Thorne (9)
St Peter's Primary School, South Croydon

Ben The Dog

Small but nice,
He does not like rice.
He likes cheese
And always smells my knees.
He sits there alone,
So he is chewing his bone.
Ben is my best friend,
But drives me round the bend.

Amy-Jane Macartney (9)
St Peter's Primary School, South Croydon

Cat And Dog Fight

The cat sat on the mat
Where it was nice and cosy
He curled up to take a nap
Suddenly, a dog came into sight
The cat went to hide
As he knew there would be a fight.

Giorgia Fennell
St Peter's Primary School, South Croydon

The Strange Door

I was walking through the trees,
Hearing the buzzing of the bees,
When I got to the shiny door,
I fell to my knees in anguish.
I was poor when I got to that door,
The buzzing of the bees
Was obviously telling me I needed keys,
So I went up to the beehive
And I got those keys from the buzzing bees.
I went to the door, opened it
And found another door!

Nicholas Peckham (9)
St Peter's Primary School, South Croydon

In My Head

In my head my sisters are driving me mad,
In my head there is the loudest siren beeping,
In my head there is a dragon blowing fire,
In my head there is a football match, England v Brazil,
In my head there is an angel teaching me to be good,
In my head there is a cricket match, England v New Zealand,
In my head there are my lovely teachers.

Beth Audus (10)
St Peter's Primary School, South Croydon

My Feelings

In my time of need,
No one would stop for me,
They would not listen to me,
I felt that I did not have a friend,
It was like no one cared,
They would not even talk to me.

Andre Kennedy-Rodney (9)
St Peter's Primary School, South Croydon

The Red Penguin

There's a penguin as red as a penguin can be,
He knocked on the window and he shouted,
'Can I buy a pet now, please?'
'Go away, we're shut.'
But he was still knocking on the door and shouting at me.
In the end I got annoyed,
So I just gave one to him through the window,
Then he came back and I thought he wanted another pet,
But he whispered to me, 'Thank you.'

George Dixon (9)
St Peter's Primary School, South Croydon

The Pink Flamingo

The pink flamingo gives you a bite,
The pink flamingo will give you a fright.
The pink flamingo will nick your food,
The pink flamingo will be in a mood.
The pink flamingo chases the mice,
The pink flamingo dives on ice.
Right now, the pink flamingo bids you goodnight,
Let's shut our eyes and sleep really tight.

Connie Grant (9)
St Peter's Primary School, South Croydon

Football

F ootball, the glorious game of football
O n my head son
O ver the bar
T ap it to me Beckham
B oot it keeper
A h, glorious football
L ovely game Ronaldo
L ovely game Rooney.

Jack Knights (9)
St Peter's Primary School, South Croydon

The Spooky School

In the dreaded spooky school
Lived creepy-crawlies and spiders
There was a boy who got dared to go in
As he stepped on the wet, slimy floor
And touched and touched the sticky walls

All he could see was cobwebs
The boys outside were waiting
The boy screamed, there was a vampire
And the boy was never seen again.

Thomas Sandle (9)
St Peter's Primary School, South Croydon

The Chief And The Thief

A thief dived in the coral reef,
But a chief saw the thief,
The chief swam after the thief,
But the chief died, oh what grief,
Sorry for this poem being so brief.

Sasha Vorontsov (7)
St Peter's Primary School, South Croydon

Angel

Angel is a person in Heaven,
Angel is sky-blue,
She is winter,
A crystal castle,
She is cold,
Angel is a silvery, sparkly ball dress,
Unicorn fall,
Healthy food.

Taylor Sidney (8)
St Peter's Primary School, South Croydon

Teddy Bears

We have two teddy bears
One big
One small
The first one has small ears
The second one has big ears
The first one has small hands
The second one has big hands
The first one has small feet
The second one has big feet
The first one has a T-shirt
The second one wears a bow.

Ashleigh Stevens (7)
St Peter's Primary School, South Croydon

Superman

Superman is red and blue
He is summery
He lives in a tall tower
He is red and blue
Superman is red and blue
He is in The Simpsons
A very nice, juicy pig's head.

Samuel Ave (8)
St Peter's Primary School, South Croydon

Fairy

Fairy is peachy pink
She is summer
Lives in a magical garden
She wears a sparkly dress
In a tall deckchair
She watches Peter Pan
And eats an icy cold, creamy ice cream.

Sade Parker (9)
St Peter's Primary School, South Croydon

Riding

Something that I really like
Is to go riding on my bike.

I like to go really fast
And my two dogs go flying past.

My bike is shiny and bright
And I ride it every night.

Thursday is the only day I don't go out
It's when Dad works at the school and he isn't about.

Cameron Warr (7)
St Peter's Primary School, South Croydon

Shimmering Princess

A princess is shimmering gold
She is as bright as a hot summer's day
She lives in a big, shiny, silver castle
She wears a sparkly pink and lilac ballgown
She has a big basket full of shoes
She absolutely adores Tracy Beaker
She loves a nice cold smoothie and a Flake.

Amira Zerrouki (9)
St Peter's Primary School, South Croydon

An Explorer

An explorer is light brown
She is the summer
In the Amazon Jungle
She is sunny
She has a hat, climbing shoes
And a jumper
Soft and cuddly
She is jungle run
And a fresh, juicy fruit salad.

David Mincer (9)
St Peter's Primary School, South Croydon

Butterfly

Butterfly, butterfly how beautiful you are,
Lots of different colours, your wings spread afar.
Summer is here, flowers are growing,
Eating the nectar, while daddies are mowing.
Brimstone, peacock and small tortoiseshell are some of their names,
Yellow, blue with black and pink with brown, we don't all look
                                                    the same.

I love the way butterflies fly,
I love the way they float in the sky,
Winter is here, it's time to say goodbye.

Mya Douglas (7)
St Peter's Primary School, South Croydon

A Witch Is . . .

A witch is black and white as night
She is the autumn
In a magical school like Hogwarts
She is bright and sunny
A witch is a school skirt and blouse
A book and wand
She is a Harry Potter or Worst Witch
The witch is a well-cooked, bursting out, toasted sandwich.

Georgia Clifton-Dey (8)
St Peter's Primary School, South Croydon

Happy As . . .

Happy as a bee to buzz, buzz, buzz
Happy as a spider to spin a web
Happy as a boy with a big bag of sweets
Happy as a fish to swim in the sea
Happy to be happy, that's me!

George Lawrence (7)
St Peter's Primary School, South Croydon

Magic

Bubble, double, toil and trouble,
Make this man into a mouble
(It means he's not going to be magic.)
Put an eye of a newt,
Then a nice big juicy flute.
Bubble, trouble, double mix,
Let's put in a chocolate bar called Twix.
Mix and turn, make it burn,
Put a piece of turnip skin,
Then put in a human chin,
Then give it to the man
And give it with a happy grin.

Rebecca Audus (7)
St Peter's Primary School, South Croydon

All About Witches

A witch is magical and sometimes mean
She is a very creamy ice cream colour
In a scarlet room
She is a summer person
Sparkly suit with polka-dots and diamonds
A sponge lover
Doctor Who
Toast with melted cheese
Macaroni, cake icing, Coca-Cola.

Daphiene Reid (8)
St Peter's Primary School, South Croydon

Superhero

Superhero is a ready fan
He is the summer
In a superhero dream cave
He is a foggy person
A ripped T-shirt with burning flames
And exciting spots
A gravity cupboard and a table
He is an Eddie Murphy fan
A delicious smell with fried chicken
And the smell of delicious chips.

Kye Clarke (8)
St Peter's Primary School, South Croydon

Angel

Angel is a person in Heaven that can fly
The angel is crystal-blue, purple and white
She is winter
A crystal castle of silver and gold
She is rainy
A yellow sparkly dress
A glass crystal tassel
Unicorn Valley of the waterfalls
Healthy food.

Ellé Barker (8)
St Peter's Primary School, South Croydon

Fire Dragon

A dragon is blazing red
(Decide if it is a she or a he)
He is summer
In a volcano
He is foggy
He is scaly
A fire-bed
He is a dragon booster
Type of food
Juicy, chunky, fat dragon.

Kelem Tahir (8)
St Peter's Primary School, South Croydon

A Healthy Superhero

Superhero is crystal-white
He is spring
He lives in an airship
He is sunny
A superhero has a white cape
And white trousers
A clean man
He is a lazy town
He eats fruit and veg.

Jack Murray (8)
St Peter's Primary School, South Croydon

Dennis The Menace

Dennis the Menace is a blurry person
He is the summer
In a dream
He is rainy
A red and black top with red shorts
A widescreen TV
He is a Dennis the Menace character
A juicy, wobbly jelly.

Maia Desaa (8)
St Peter's Primary School, South Croydon

The Black Witch

A witch is black
She is the winter
In a dark wood
She is misty
A black cloak
A glass table
She is a Simpson
A frog's leg.

Hannah Pettengale (8)
St Peter's Primary School, South Croydon

Shopkeeper

A shopkeeper is orangey-red
He is autumn when the leaves all fall
In a snazzy, sky-high shop
He is sunny-bright
A shopkeeper is an overall with gold buttons
A vanity table with mirrors in every direction
He is The Crust
A mayonnaisey tuna salad.

Chloe Lewis (8)
St Peter's Primary School, South Croydon

A Time Traveller

A time traveller is sapphire-blue
She is the leafy autumn
She is a time machine
She is misty
She is a high-heeled boot
A cinema screen
She is Doctor Who
A chocolate bar
A creamy, caramel chocolate bar.

Hannah Darkes (9)
St Peter's Primary School, South Croydon

My Pirate Trip

On my pirate ship
I went on a very long trip,
Drinking rum
To warm up my tum,
I said, 'Ho, ho, ho and here we go,
To the island of gold.'

Max Nichols (7)
St Peter's Primary School, South Croydon

Doctor Who

Who are you
Doctor Who?
Travelling in your
TARDIS blue.

Travelling in space
And back in time
Meeting up with old friends
Like K9.

Battling enemies
Old and new
Daleks, Sycorax and Cybermen
To name but a few.

Rose Tyler is a
Very good friend
Helped to fight
The Slitheen to the end.

Werewolves, clockwork robots
And the Empty Child
Doctor Who fights them all
And drives them wild!

Doctor Who is only
In our imagination
But has captured
The hearts of the nation!

Elsa Hunter (7)
St Peter's Primary School, South Croydon

Formula One

It's Sunday afternoon, I am watching TV,
Now's the time for the Japanese Grand Prix.
My favourite is Alonso in yellow and blue,
Mummy likes Jensen, what about you?

I stare at the screen as they race round the bend,
Oh when, oh when will they reach the end?
There are races in Italy, Belgium and France,
They have got to be fast to be in with a chance.
At speeds of over 200 miles an hour,
The engines have got to have lots of power.

Come on Fernando, you've got to go fast,
Oh, please don't let Schumacher get past!
I don't want Ferrari, just Benetton Renault,
Go on Alonso, put your foot down and go!

It's near the end now, just one more lap
And Michael is trying to close the gap.
But what's happened now? He's started to spin,
Alonso is speeding, he is going to win.
Ferrari's engine has blown, he won't win today
And I am cheering and shouting hooray!

As fast as you can now, round the last bend,
Just up ahead, you can now see the end.
There it is, the chequered flag,
Alonso has won and it's time to brag.
He drove with skill and was the best,
Today he was miles better than the rest.

You're number one, go get the cup,
Get onto the podium and lift it right up.
Cover the others with champagne spray,
I am so happy my team won today!

Thomas W F Dixon (7)
St Peter's Primary School, South Croydon

The Life Cycle Of A Frog

They usually begin life in water as eggs.
When are they going to grow legs?
A ball of jelly surrounds each of the eggs,
Which are called spawn, or you can call it frogs-born.

After ten days, the tadpole hatches
And wiggles out of the jelly ball.
I wonder if tadpoles crawl?
These tadpoles breathe through gills that are on the outside.
How come they are not inside?

Gradually the back legs begin to appear
And the outside gills begin to disappear.
Do the gills reappear?
One week after the legs form,
The tadpole develops lungs and can breathe air.
How long is its hair?

Then in 10 to 12 weeks, tadpole develops front legs.
I wonder if they eat nutmegs?
After its front legs form, the tadpole does not eat,
But absorbs its tail for food.
I hope its nails are gone for good.

At about three and a half months it becomes a froglet
And can eat small bugs.
I hope they get lots of hugs.
It now spends its time out of the water,
It had better have a cousin called Mater.

Once the frog finishes growing and has lost its tail,
It is considered an adult frog.
I bet they're soon going to be jumping on logs.

Sashawne Smith (7)
St Peter's Primary School, South Croydon

The Dark Night Sky

The soft wind blows in the dark night sky,
The stars are twinkling way up high,
The moon is bright,
Not a cloud in sight,
The background is coloured with an indigo-blue.

The owls are hooting in the trees,
The foxes scampering through the leaves,
The bats are swooping,
The badgers are stomping,
The rabbit likes what he sees.

The people are sleeping in their beds,
The pillow comforts their sleepy heads,
Some of them dream,
Some of them snore,
They lie still, as if they are dead.

The grass is white and hard with frost,
The bricks are covered with icy moss,
The road is sparkling,
The pavement is slippery,
The cat slinks by just like a ghost.

When I look out of my window,
I am amazed by what I see below,
It makes me smile,
It makes me think,
Of a picture I saw long ago.

Now the sun is rising high
And the sky above is really bright,
The night has ended,
The day is here,
I will never forget what I saw last night.

Anna Mapstone (7)
St Peter's Primary School, South Croydon

Hannah's Ballet Class

I love my ballet classes,
I go there every week,
I turn and twist and twirl,
With my pink ballet shoes on my feet.

I wear a blue leotard,
A belt and cardigan too,
I wear a headband on my head
And wear pink socks in my shoe.

My hair is pulled back,
In a beautiful ballet bun,
With a hairnet and lots of clips,
This is all part of the fun.

My teacher is called Miss Amanda,
I learn at Gresham School,
I go to ballet on Fridays
And I dance in the school hall.

I once did a solo,
In front of a large crowd,
They were cheering and clapping
And they seemed really loud.

I once went on stage,
It was nice and bright,
I danced so nicely,
Everybody said what a lovely sight.

Hannah Penn (7)
St Peter's Primary School, South Croydon

My Weather Poem

When it rains
My boots I wear
I splash in puddles
And I don't care!

When it's sunny
I get hot
I feel like
I'm in a cooking pot!

When it's windy
The cold wind blows
Help! It gives me
Frozen toes!

When it snows
It gets icy
So I want
Some food that's spicy.

When it's stormy
Flashing lightning
And claps of thunder
Are very frightening.

When it's cloudy
The sky is grey
So you don't want
To go out and play.

Lucy Taylor (7)
St Peter's Primary School, South Croydon